SECRETS
THE GREAT OLD-TIMEY COOKS
BY
BARBARA SWELL

Photo courtesy of Ferrum College, Virginia

ISBN: 978-1-883206-37-6   Order No. NGB-830
Library of Congress Control Number: 2001087782
©2001 by Native Ground Music, Inc.
Asheville, North Carolina
International Copyright Secured. All Rights Reserved.
Printed in Canada

INTRODUCTION

We all know who the great old-timey cooks are. The women who know how to make anything taste good. They grew up during lean times in the 1920s and 30s on rural farms. Their day started at 5:00 a.m. with chores done by lantern-light, meals cooked on the wood cook stove, food refrigerated in the spring house, and water carried to the kitchen in buckets.

There's a fire that still burns bright in the soul of these great cooks. They can make a quilt out of cigar labels and reuse the string from feed sacks to crochet lace. They can milk the cows, hoe the corn, cut the tobacco, and kill, dress, and cook the hen for dinner. Even though the great old-timey cooks can now go buy their groceries at the well-stocked local market, they prefer to eat from their kitchen gardens. They grow and can the best tomatoes, their beans are shiny and bursting with flavor, and they pick their cucumbers at the perfect time to make their famous pickles.

You know what the great cook will bring to the church supper, and everybody clamors for her special dish, which is the first to get eaten. She learned to cook from her mother, and she from hers. Her darkened tin baking pans have advertising logos imprinted in them. Of course, she always makes the apple butter in the same pan. That way there's no need to measure ingredients.

Trade card courtesy Jimmy Greene

Someone once asked my grandmother as a child, "Are you a Methodist or a Baptist?" Being almost as wise at five as she was at 95, she replied, "I'm just plain folks." She said that about her cooking too, "nothing fancy," but anyone who ate her food knew better. My grandmother's gone, but she's in the room with me whenever I make her chicken pie. My sisters and I gleaned every cooking secret from her we could. I hope you'll do the same with the great old-timey cooks in your life, because when they're gone, there'll be no other generation like theirs. I am grateful to the women who allowed me to interview them for this book, generously sharing their cooking secrets, recipes, and stories. These ladies are true treasures.

CONTENTS

Photo courtesy Great Smoky Mountains National Park

THE GREAT COOKS

EFFIE PRICE

I met Effie after we bought and restored the cabin where she grew up. She was born in 1914, and raised in Big Pine, North Carolina, in the heart of the beautiful Appalachian mountains. Her grandfather built their hand-hewn log cabin in about 1890 on the side of the steep mountain where she and her family lived a self-sufficient life. They farmed for their food, milked the cows, raised hogs, and chickens, and bought only staples like baking soda, salt, and coffee at the local store. Tobacco and sweet potato crops brought in income enough to buy what little was needed. Oil lanterns provided light, and a mule-powered wagon provided transportation.

Effie is a wonderful cook. Each time I see her, she loads me up with gifts from her kitchen: delicious apple butter, pickles, or crabapple jelly. She makes beauti-

Young Effie and her mother

ful old-timey quilts and also crochets. I feel Effie's kind and spirited presence every time I stand in her old kitchen and reach into the wood cook stove for a pan of hot, fluffy buttermilk biscuits.

Photo by Wayne Erbsen, January, 2001

Effie's cabin home in Big Pine, N.C. from 1914-1938

THE GREAT COOKS

GELEMA WORLEY

Several people were gathered around the end of the long metal table obstructing my view. This being my first time at the annual Big Pine fire department fundraising auction, I figured there must

Gelema Worley

be something special over there. When I finally made my way over, I saw the apple stack cake, along with some other good looking cakes and pies just waiting to be auctioned. I heard someone say, "Gelema sure makes a fine cake." Several others nodded, and I knew I'd have to hunt her down and see if she'd share her cake secrets with me.

Now, you might think that someone who's as famous as Gelema is for her stack cake might hold tight to her recipe, but not this friendly and talented woman. The second oldest of nine children who grew up in a rural mountain farm community, Gelema's a "made from scratch" cook who says, "I've never bought a box of biscuits in my life." She told me how to cook a coon with onion and red hot pepper, which vegetable seeds to buy, and shared her ideas about the old days. Like all the women I spoke with, Gelema remembers growing up working hard without modern amenities and sewing hand-made clothes cut from patterned feed sacks. She says, "Those were good times because people helped each other out. They'd sit up with you all night if you were sick. People were happy."

A mountain cornfield...fall view from Gelema's front porch.

THE GREAT COOKS

JUANITA (NITA) STACKHOUSE

When I asked my friend, Will Pruett, a Methodist preacher in rural Madison County, N.C. for the names of some great old-timey cooks, he said, "Go see Nita Stackhouse. She can make anything taste good." Now, Will has probably eaten home cooking at more church suppers than just about anybody, so I took his advice and went to see Nita.

My husband, Wayne, and I followed the long, winding gravel road to the breathtakingly beautiful, secluded valley where she lives. We found her in the kitchen of her lovely Victorian home perched on the side of a mountain, overlooking the misty French Broad River. Feeling like we had known her for years, she gave us more than the recipes we asked for. She told us of growing up on a farm in Charlotte, N.C., and how she met, fell in love, and married her husband, Gilbert. She even gave us advice on what makes love last (see page 47 for specifics.) Nita reminds me of what I've always known: great old-timey cooks have big hearts.

Photo by Wayne Erbsen

Nita Stackhouse shares her cooking secrets with the author.

My daddy's grandmother used to tell him, "You pick the berries and I'll make a pie special for just you."

THE GREAT COOKS

MARGARET WORLEY

Margaret and her husband Ray, were resting from handing (sorting) their tobacco harvest when I went to visit them. Their Big Pine, N.C. home and land is as pictur-esque as any you've ever seen. Ray helped his father build the farmhouse, barn, cellar house, and other out-buildings in the early 1940's before he and Margaret were married.

Margaret Worley

Margaret learned to cook from her grandmother, who lived with her family while she was growing up in nearby Barnard. She remembers buying fabric to sew their clothes from the local grocery. This store also carried shoes, hardware, and anything else you could want in addition to the staples needed to supplement what the farmers could grow for their families.

Not only can she cook, but Margaret still sews up a storm as well. During the winter months, while the garden rests, you'll find her piecing and stitching beautiful traditional quilts that sell as fast as she can make them.

ETTA

Etta is long gone, I'm sure. I bought her hand-written cookbook from someone in Massachusetts through an on-line auction. Of little value to collectors, the book is coverless, yellowed, brittle, faded, and in terrible shape. But a closer look reveals pieces of the life of a New England woman who knew how to cook. From rusted magazine and newspaper clippings, penciled-in notes, and lots of pamphlets, here's what I've gleaned about Etta:

Her cooking is clearly New England style with a southern influence. Perhaps she or her relatives lived in the South. Etta began the book in about 1906 and continued it until at least 1918. She grew a vegetable garden, had strong ties with family, and entertained occasionally, but probably not frequently. One day I'll transcribe this manuscript. It contains the best collection of recipes I've ever seen. If you have a treasure like this in your family, I hope you'll pass it along as an heirloom; and please jot down a few notes about the author to stick in the book with all the other clippings!

THE WOOD COOK STOVE

Y ou haven't truly lived unless you've tasted a home-made apple pie that's been baked in a wood cook stove. Though not commonplace today, just about every homemaker owned a stove by the turn of the twentieth century. American manufacture of cast iron cooking ranges began in the 1820s. The design evolved over time from a "step-top" with the oven on top, to the more familiar range with the oven below and warming compartments above.

By the late 1840s, iron cooking stoves were becoming popular among residents of the eastern and midsections of the country. Even housewives embarking on the Oregon trail were reluctant to resume life on the frontier without their trusty stoves. Little wonder, though, that the weighty iron monsters were the first thing to be discarded alongside the trail when the going got tough. Western settlers again resorted to hearth cooking until the stoves could be shipped by rail in the late 1860s.

Canning beans on a Majestic steel wood-fired range.

Photo courtesy of Mars Hill College

THE WOOD COOK STOVE

While there are countless reasons not to cook with a wood range today, I'll tell you some of the delights. The main one is that it will slow the pace of your life. Though you can get a cold cook stove fired up quick enough to boil water in 15 minutes if you use the right wood, chances are good that you'll want to savor the experience and cook while the stove's hot. Especially if you find yourself in a drafty antique log cabin in the mountains on a frosty winter morning.

So here's what you do: stack the grate with kindling, start the fire, put your coffee on the stove to perk, and step outside onto the back porch. Grab your axe and split some dry, aged oak, hickory, or locust into one and two inch wide pieces and head back to the stove. You're warm now and your coffee's ready. Add the hardwood to your fire, and whip up some biscuits. Close the flue

damper so hot air circulates around the firebox, and put your biscuits in the oven. As you fry up your eggs, bacon, and apples, rotate the biscuits. Otherwise, the ones nearest the firebox will burn. Right about now, you may want to put those beans you soaked last night in a pan and start to slow-simmer them on the back of the stove for supper tonight. Now open the damper, add a little more wood to keep the kitchen warm, dish up your food, and put it in the warming oven while you set the table and call in your guests.

Photo courtesy Library of Congress

BEVERAGES

RUSSIAN TEA

4 Tbs. tea leaves
10 whole cloves
1 cup sugar
½ gallon boiling water

3 sticks cinnamon
Juice of 2 oranges.
Juice of ½ lemon

Pour boiling water over tea, sugar, cinnamon, and cloves. Let stand 10 minutes. Strain and add fruit juices. Serve hot.

SADIE'S PUNCH

"Every time I served this punch when entertaining, the guests came back for a second cup!"

Nita Stackhouse

2 cups sugar
6 cups water
¼ cup pineapple juice

½ cup lemon juice
1½ cups orange juice
2 bottles ginger ale

Bring to a boil 1 cup water, add sugar and let cool. Add fruit juices and remaining water. Just before serving, add ginger ale. Serve on ice. Better yet, pour a couple inches of water into a tube pan, add chunks of pineapple and cherries, if you have them, then freeze and float the frozen ring on top of the punch.

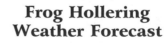

Frog Hollering Weather Forecast

When frogs holler, rain will soon foller.

When a frog hollers in the spring, it's a sign that winter has ended.[20]

BEVERAGES

MAE'S DANDELION WINE

"In the dewy morning, pick one qt. (packed tight) of fresh opened dandelion blossoms. Pour over them one gallon of boiling water and let stand for 24 hours in an old 5 gallon stone crock. Remove blossoms, add 4 lbs. granulated sugar, one lemon cut fine, and one package yeast. Let this stand at room temperature for 36 hours, stirring well occasionally. Strain through double thickness of cheese cloth and bottle. Put cheese cloth on bottle tops and let stand in cool place until bubbles stop. Seal. When the wine has aged for two years, it's time to invite the ladies for tea."[7]

Autograph Rhyme, 1891

Dear Georgetta,

If wisdom's ways you'd wisely keep,
Five things observe with care:
Of whom you speak, to whom you speak,
And how, and when, and where.

Your friend and teacher, Mrs. Adams
March 21, 1891, Muddy Creek Forks

BLACKBERRY CORDIAL

Photo courtesy Library of Congress

"Pick as many large blackberries as you can. Mash and strain through cheesecloth without heating them. To every quart of juice add one pound of sugar. Tie in thick muslin bag, ½ oz. of grated nutmeg, ¼ oz. whole cinnamon, ¼ oz. whole cloves and one small piece of mace. Boil juice and spices 25 minutes, removing scum as it rises. Remove spice bag and stir in 4 tablespoons vanilla extract. Pour syrup into hot jars and seal."[9]

BEVERAGES

Photo courtesy North Dakota State University

GRAPE JUICE LEMONADE

4 lemons	1 pint grape juice
3 cups water	½ cup sugar (or to taste)

Mix all ingredients and heat until sugar dissolves. Serve chilled over ice with sliced lemon wedges.

MULLED CIDER

½ gallon apple cider	¼ cup packed brown sugar
Juice of 1 lemon	2 cinnamon sticks
Juice of 4 oranges	8 whole cloves and allspice

Combine all ingredients and simmer 15 minutes. Remove spices, add some thinly sliced lemon and oranges, and serve hot.

Anybody born while the mulberries are ripe has a good chance of being red-headed.

12

SOUPS

SNOWDRIFT TOMATO BISQUE

This recipe comes from Snowdrift's 1913 shortening cookbook. Old advertising cookbooklets are a rich source of American food nostalgia. They're often stuffed with newspaper clippings and hand-written recipes that give you a glimpse into an earlier life. Pick them up at yard sales, through on-line auctions, and from your own older relatives.

6 fresh, ripe tomatoes	2 Tbs. Snowdrift shortening
1 bay leaf	1 blade (pinch) mace
4 Tbs. flour	1 slice of onion
1 tsp. salt	3 cups milk
Dash cayenne	

Cook onion in a little butter until translucent. Dip tomatoes in boiling water a minute to loosen skins. Chop skinned tomatoes and add to onion along with the mace, bay leaf, and salt. In a small skillet, melt shortening; add flour, then a dab of milk, stirring all until you have a smooth paste. Gradually add the rest of the milk. Stir over medium heat until smooth and thickened. Pour the tomatoes into a tureen, then hastily add the thickened milk. Stir and send at once to the table.[14]

*Note: You can use canned, chopped tomatoes; just omit the salt. Substitute a dash of nutmeg if you don't have any ground mace.

Photo courtesy of US Department of Agriculture

SOUPS

OLD FASHIONED DRIED CORN CHOWDER

Slowly simmer ½ cup dried sweet corn in 2 cups water for about an hour until tender. Add a large diced sweet potato, ½ of a chopped purple onion, 2 minced cloves of garlic, and a cup of water or chicken broth. Simmer for about 30 minutes more, then add a can of creamed corn and a cup of milk (not skim.) Heat 5 minutes, but don't boil. Add fresh or dried herbs, and salt and pepper to taste. Serve topped with grated yellow cheddar cheese and a sprig of fresh parsley or cilantro. **Note:** See page 69 for dried corn source.

Vegetable Insults

- *His family is like potatoes, all that is good of them is underground.*[18]
- *She's like a fly on a collard (light headed and restless.)*
- *She rattles around her house like one pea in a pod.*
- *He's too lazy to shuck corn if you gave it to him.*[17]

Photo courtesy of Alice Lloyd College

SOUPS

ETTA'S CELERY SOUP

"Cook 3 cups finely chopped celery until tender. Add celery to one quart of hot milk. Salt to taste. Rub a little flour smooth with butter and add one cup of mashed potato. Serve very hot with squares of toast."

Log corn "crib-shed" used for drying ears of field corn.

"One of Alex Cole's children."
Johnnie Otto (p. 44) was her cousin.

ETTA'S GARDEN FRESH GREEN PEA SOUP

"2 qts. of fresh green peas cooked in a very little water. When tender, rub through a collander. Add to pulp an equal quantity of milk and an onion. Season to taste, simmer, remove onion."

Note: Frozen peas are a good substitute for fresh. Cook as directed above, and put through a food mill or blend in a food processor. Season with salt, pepper, a sprinkle of nutmeg, and either thyme or tarragon (fresh is best if you have it.)

- A fat kitchen, a lean will.
- A rotten apple spoils its companion.
- Beauty cannot compensate for want of heart.
- Beauty and folly are old companions.
- First thrive and then wive.
- Don't fall out with your bread and butter.[18]

BREADS

There are as many recipes for cornbread as there are cooks. If you live in the South, you use white self-rising cornmeal and you don't add any sugar. Up North and elsewhere, folks prefer a sweeter cornbread using yellow meal. Regardless of where you live, there's a cornbread that's just right for you. Use fresh stone-ground meal, if possible, and keep it refrigerated so the oil in the germ doesn't spoil.

SOUTHERN MOUNTAIN CORNBREAD

Margaret Worley of Big Pine, N.C. uses a recipe similar to this, but she adds a little water to the milk and omits the egg; and like most good cooks, she doesn't measure. She makes her cornbread in a square pan because her husband Ray, likes the corners. "He'll eat every one of the corners if I let him!" Many Southerners, including Ray, prefer to break their cornbread instead of cutting it with a knife.

2 cups self-rising cornmeal   ¼ cup melted shortening
1 ¼ cups milk   1 egg (optional)

Preheat oven to 450°. Melt butter in a cast iron skillet. Beat the egg with the milk, and add melted butter. Stir in the cornmeal until just combined (don't overbeat) Pour batter into hot, buttered skillet and bake about 25 minutes until browned.

Ray helps Margaret hold up one of the beautiful traditional quilts she sews.

Photo by Wayne Erbsen

16

BREADS

Photo courtesy of Mars Hill College

GRITTED CORN BREAD

The woman in this photo is gritting corn with a home made grater crafted especially for this purpose. You grit corn when it looks dry but has a little of the milk still left in it. This makes a tasty, moist cornbread. If you don't grow your own corn, just buy some that looks like it's drying out, husk it, and air dry it for about a week.

1 cup gritted corn meal	½ cup white flour
2 tsp. baking powder	3 Tbs. melted butter
1 tsp. salt	Milk to make a thin batter

Preheat oven to 450°. Combine corn meal, baking powder, salt, flour, and stir. Add butter and enough milk to make a batter just thin enough to pour. Pour into a hot, buttered iron skillet. Bake until lightly browned.

> *Corn meal that's not dried out makes stubborn bread.*
> *Corn is not ready to grind into meal until it's dry as an old maid's kiss.*[18]

BREADS

BISCUITS

Your biscuits will be as good as the flour you use to make them. I use White Lilly or Big Spring Mill's self-rising flour. These are popular here in the South and by mail (see pg. 69 for mail ordering information). There are many fine flours available. Try them all! For tender, flaky biscuits purchase those made from soft winter wheat.

2 cups self-rising flour	Whole or buttermilk
5 Tbs. butter or shortening	(¼ tsp. soda if buttermilk)

Cut shortening into flour (the best cooks use their hands). Add enough milk to make a soft dough you can handle. Knead a minute, then roll out on a floured board one inch thick. Cut with a sharp biscuit cutter straight down. Don't twist. Place in a buttered pan and bake in a preheated 450° oven until lightly browned. Send to the table hot with butter and home-made jam.

Photo courtesy of Library of Congress

"Better the guests wait on the biscuits than the biscuits wait on the guests!"

BREADS

JAM WINDMILLS

2 cups flour
3 tsp. baking powder
1 tsp. salt
2 Tbs. sugar

4 Tbs. butter
1 egg
½ cup milk

Sift flour, baking powder, salt, and sugar together. Rub butter into the mixture. Beat egg and add milk, then stir into flour mixture. Add more milk if needed until you have a soft dough you can roll out. Turn out on a floured board and knead a minute. Roll into a rectangular shape about ¼ inch thick. Cut into 3 inch squares. Cut diagonally from each corner to the center. Fold every other corner toward the center, pinwheel style. Punch your thumb into the middle of the pinwheel to close, leaving a big hole. Bake on a buttered cookie sheet in a 450° preheated oven until lightly browned (about 10 minutes or so). Invite your guests to fill the thumb holes with some of your home-made jam.

HUCKLEBERRY SCONES

Make Windmill dough as above and fold in ½ cup fresh picked huckleberries or 1 cup blueberries after you've added the milk. Divide into two balls and roll each out into a circle about 1 inch thick. Slice into wedges and sprinkle with coarse sugar. Bake as above.

Huckleberries

We huckleberry gatherers don't like to admit it, but what we call huckleberries are actually mountain blueberries. Found in many mountainous regions of the country growing wild, they are small, bluish-black, and have an intense blueberry flavor. We pick them in mid to late August off the beautiful Blue Ridge Parkway here in the North Carolina mountains. Check the agricultural extension office in the mountains near you to find out where they grow and when they ripen.

BREADS

W ho would have guessed that graham flour (coarsely ground whole wheat flour) had such a colorful past? It was named after Sylvester Graham. He was born in 1794, the youngest of seventeen children. Having been a puny child, he became interested in nutritional wellness at a time when Americans tended to be gluttonous eaters of meat, fat, starches,

and sweets. Bakers began using refined flour in their breads. Fresh, raw fruits and vegetables were blamed for cholera epidemics and rarely made it to table of the average urban diner in the early 1800s.

Graham became a professional reformer, imploring people to abstain from meat, refined grains, alcohol, caffeine, spicy foods, and sweets. He also encouraged folks to get lots of sunshine, fresh air, and to avoid frequent sex. It's no surprise that bakers, butchers, and amorous couples were outraged by

Sylvester Graham

Graham's teachings. Around the time he invented the graham cracker in 1829, he did have, however, quite a large following of "Grahamites", who lived in Graham boarding houses and followed his diet.

Late 19th and early 20th century cookbooks are filled with recipes for graham breads and cakes. Any whole-wheat flour will work in these recipes, but your results will be more authentic if you use coarsely ground whole wheat flour available from historic mills or health markets.

Photo, author's collection

The graham recipes that follow come verbatim from the 1906-18 hand-written cookbook of a New England woman named Etta. As with most good cooks, Etta's recipes are vague. She only needed to know the ingredients in a recipe because she knew what to do from that point. Little did this wonderful Massachusetts cook know that 95 years later many of her recipes would be published. Following each recipe I've added directions for baking.

BREADS

RAISIN GRAHAM BREAD

3 cups of graham flour
3 teaspoons of baking powder
1 cup milk and ½ cup water

¼ cup sugar
1 cup raisins
1 tsp. salt

"Let stand in warm place ½ hour. Nutmeats may be used."

Combine 1 cup milk, ½ cup water, sugar, salt (I would use 1½ tsp. salt), chopped walnuts, and raisins. Stir in baking powder until mixed, then add graham flour until you have a dough that sticks together enough to handle. Put onto a lightly (white) floured surface and knead a minute. Form it into a flattened ball, then let it sit for ½ hour in a warm place. Bake on a baking stone or buttered cookie sheet at 350° until lightly browned and cooked through. Serve hot from the oven.

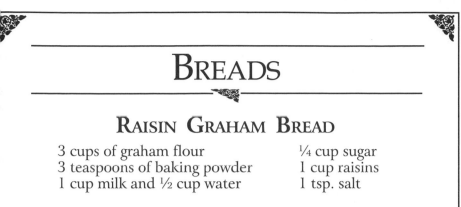

Dough Warnings

Bread dough turns sad if it sits too long. (Sad is an old-timey term for soggy.)

If you don't share your dough, your bread won't rise.[18]

GRAHAM PUFFS

1 cup of sour milk, 1 tablespoon of molasses, 1 spoonful of salt, 1 teaspoonful of soda. Graham flour to make a dough that's quite stiff. Bake in buttered gem-tins.

19th century cast iron gem pan

These were often called Graham Gems. Heat a cast iron gem pan, if you have one, then butter each while hot. Pour batter into pan right away and bake in a 375° oven until lightly browned. You can use a muffin or mini-muffin pan as well. This recipe is rather salty if baked as written. You can omit most of the salt.

BREADS

FANNIE'S GRAHAM BREAD

1 cup of sour milk
½ cup sweet milk
2 Tbs. of molasses
2 Tbs. of sugar

Pinch of salt
1 tsp. soda
2 cups of graham flour
½ cup wheat (white) flour

My guess is that you combine all the wet ingredients, sift the dry, then combine the two. Put dough into a greased loaf pan and bake at 350° about 40 minutes or until browned for a heavy, hearty loaf.

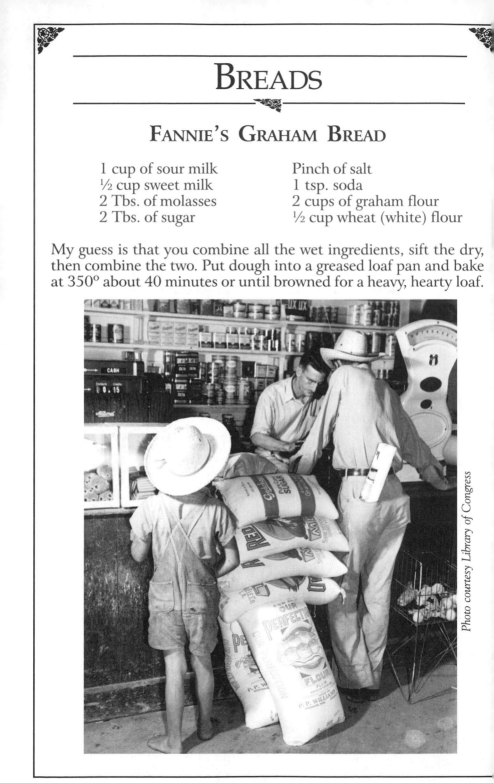

Photo courtesy Library of Congress

Breads

Mary Randolph's 1824 Sweet Potato Buns

"Boil and mash a large sweet potato, rub into it as much flour as will make it like bread. Add spice and sugar to your taste, with a spoonful of yeast. When it has risen well, work in a piece of butter; bake it in small rolls, to be eaten hot with butter, either for breakfast or tea."[13]

Florida State Archives

Note: This recipe calls for no liquid other than a spoonful of yeast (which would have been in liquid form.) Though not true to Mary's recipe, you can dissolve a package of powdered yeast in ¼ cup of milk, add cooled mashed sweet potato, a spoonful or two of brown sugar, a piece of softened butter, ½ tsp. salt, and a pinch of cinnamon and nutmeg. Add flour to make a dough you can handle, and knead it like any bread dough. Let rise until doubled, punch down, and make it into small rolls. Place in a buttered pan to rise a bit, then bake in a preheated 375° oven until browned.

Dwayne's Sweet Potato Dumplings

Effie Price learned to make these old-timey dumplings from her grandson, Dwayne Finley. She taught him to make biscuits when Dwayne was so small that he had to stand on a chair to reach the counter.

Make biscuits (pg. 18) and cut dough out into circles. Roll each biscuit thin and put some mashed sweet potatoes in the center of each one. Bring the sides of the biscuit up around the filling, so that just a little potato peeks out in the middle. Crimp biscuit like you would a pie crust. Meanwhile, boil 3 cups water with 1½ cups sugar (white or ½ white and ½ brown). Pour ½ of the boiling syrup into a large rectangular baking dish and carefully place the dumplings on top, being careful that the syrup does not cover them. Pour the rest of the syrup around the sides of the biscuits, if there's room. Sprinkle cinnamon and a little nutmeg on top. Bake at 350° for 25 or 30 minutes until browned.

Note: These taste great without the syrup if you're watching your intake of sweets. Just omit syrup and bake like you would biscuits in a buttered pan.

BREADS

Photo courtesy Library of Congress

Bread Weather Forecast

- *To take the last piece of bread on a plate foretells rain.*
- *If you drop a piece of buttered bread upside down on the floor, it will soon rain.*
- *If, handling a loaf of bread, it breaks into two parts, it'll rain all week.*[20]

MEATS

WOOD COOK STOVE BLACKBIRD PIE

"Dress and cleanse well a dozen blackbirds as you would pigeons. Split each in half, put them into stew pan with plenty of water and bring to boiling point; then add salt and pepper to season, some minced parsley, a chopped onion, and about 3 whole cloves. Add about 1 cup diced salt pork. Thicken broth with browned flour and boil up. Add 2 cups diced potatoes; grease baking dish, and put in alternate layers of birds and potatoes, cover with broth and then a rich pastry crust. Slit top crust and bake in oven until cooked and browned."[16]   Home Comfort Cook Book, 1933

PORK SNOW BIRDS

Mix together one and one half pounds of ground pork shoulder, one cup of uncooked white rice, an onion chopped fine, salt, pepper and form into balls. Place in a skillet, pour in one pint tomatoes (marinara sauce adds more flavor), two cups boiling water, and simmer two hours, keeping the skillet covered. You can also bake this in the oven in a covered casserole dish. Serve hot.[2]

MEATS

ROAST BEEF PIE WITH POTATO CRUST, 1915

Chop cold, cooked meat, and place in a glass casserole dish. To each cup of meat pour in one-third cup gravy or one-fourth cup water. Add salt and pepper to taste, some finely chopped onion, and a little parsley. Spread mashed potatoes as a crust over the meat; bake in a 350° oven until golden brown and bubbly.[8]

Courtesy Library of Congress

How To Cook Beefsteak, 1872

Pound well your meat until the fibres break,
Be sure that next you have, to broil the steak,
Good coal in plenty; nor a moment leave,
But turn it over this way, and then that;
The lean should be quite rare, not so the fat.
The platter now and then the juice receive,
Put on your butter, place it on your meat;
Salt, pepper, turn it over, serve and eat.

Mrs. Winslow's Domestic Receipt Book

MEATS

HOT POT, 1910 (ETTA)

Cut up meat and rub in flour. Cut potatoes in small pieces. Put potatoes first in bottom of dish, a layer of meat, and a layer of onions and seasoning. Continue layering until dish is full, ending with potatoes on top. Pour cold water over until dish is nearly full, and bake 3 hours.

Note: You can make this dish with boneless pork, chicken breast, or sliced beef. Slice potatoes thickly (one per serving.) Slice onions as directed in recipe, and season with thyme, salt, and pepper. Add only about a cup of water, cover dish with foil or oven proof lid, and bake at 325° for about 1½ hours. Check after 1 hour to see if it's done.

Courtesy of David Anderson   Photo by Gideon Laney

TO MAKE OYSTER LOAVES, 1824

*This recipe comes verbatim from Mary Randolph's cookbook, **The Virginia House-wife**. She was a terrific early American cook, and her recipes are to this day innovative and timeless. You can serve any kind of cream based soup or stew in individual bread bowls. She used the bread to thicken the*

stew; you may thicken yours as she did, or you can mix a bit of flour with cream or milk before heating.

"Take little round loaves, cut off the top, scrape out all the crumbs, then put the oysters into a stew pan with the crumbs that came out of the loaves, a little water, and a good lump of butter; stew them together ten or fifteen minutes, then put in a spoonful of good cream, fill your loaves, lay the bit of crust carefully on again, set them in the oven to crisp. Three are enough for a side dish."

Meats

Photo courtesy Library of Congress

Cajun woman hulling rice, 1938

Curried Chicken & Rice

"Fry in the pot you make the curry in, three slices of bacon, 2 onions; cut up the chicken in small pieces, slice 3 large potatoes, put in with pork and onions, cover with water and cook until done; salt and pepper. Put 3 tablespoons of curry powder, mix with water, boil and dish over boiled rice. Serve with green peas or young corn."

Carolina Rice Cookbook, 1901

Note: The pork that the recipe refers to is the bacon you fried up. Also, I would taste the sauce after each tablespoon of curry powder you add, as these combinations of spices differ greatly in strength.

MEATS

NITA'S CHICKEN AND DUMPLINGS

There's nothing special about the ingredients in this heart-warming dish. It's the deft hand of the cook that makes this a meal that loved ones clamor for. Nita Stackhouse, now 95, has made a lot of Chicken and Dumplings in her time. She's a well-respected cook and a much loved friend to many in the N.C. mountains where she lives. I'd listen to her if I were you.

"Boil a baking hen a long time. You want to salt the broth to taste and let it simmer until the meat falls from the bones. Keep a good amount of broth in the pan. We used to leave the bones in the pot and eat around them, but you can take them out if you want before you add the dumplings."

Dumplings:

2 cups flour	3 Tbs. shortening
½ tsp. salt	Pinch of baking soda

Work above ingredients together, then add chicken broth to make a firm dough. Knead the dough until it holds together and roll out ¼ inch thick on a floured board. Nita cuts her dumplings about 2 inches long and 1 inch wide. Now, here's the artistic part: "Drop the dumplings in the simmering broth, cover the pot, and cook as long as you want. The secret to the noodles not sticking together is making your dough real stiff."

Photo courtesy of Florida State Archives

Note: If you've had good Chicken and Dumplings and you know how to throw food together well, this recipe is all you need. For the rest of you, find someone like Nita who can show you how to cook this dish and who isn't shy about sharing her her culinary talents and some stories as well!

MEATS

Photo courtesy of Berea College, Kentucky

WILD APPLE MAPLE DUCK

1 wild duck   4 strips bacon
½ cup raisins   6 oranges
3 firm apples, peeled and sliced into wedges
Real maple syrup

Combine the apples and raisins and stuff into duck cavity. Place the duck in a roasting pan, cover the breasts with bacon strips (you can secure strips with tooth picks.) Pour strained juice of oranges and ¼ cup maple syrup over the duck. Bake at 350° until done, basting frequently. Cover with foil if it's browning too fast. If nobody's going to hunt you a duck, you can substitute a whole chicken with good results. Follow package directions for cooking times.

Fashionable duck dining attire, 1890's

VEGETABLES

WINTER SACCATASH, 1846

"This is a mixture of dried beans and hard Indian corn. Take equal quantities of shelled beans and corn that has been removed from the cob and dried. Put them over-night into separate pans, and pour boiling water over them. Let them soak until morning. Then pour off that water, and scald them again. First boil the beans by themselves, as they require more cooking than the corn. Then take some cold pork or bacon, cut it into small slips. Put it with the corn into a clean pot of boiling water and let all boil together until the corn is quite soft. Lastly, drain out the water. Add some pepper. Send the saccatash to table in a tureen or a deep dish."[10]

Note: What Eliza Leslie referred to as Saccatash in 1846, we now call Succotash.

FRIED CORN

Photo courtesy of Ferrum College, Va.

Fry a piece of bacon in a skillet. Pour out the grease, but leave just enough to coat the pan. Cut sweet corn from cobs and throw it in the hot skillet. Cook on medium-high heat about 5 minutes, stirring frequently, until kernels begin to brown. You can toss in a pinch of sugar, but if your corn's good and fresh, you won't need to. Crumble the bacon and toss it in with the corn, sprinkle with pepper, and send it to the table.

Corn Sayins

- *We're eatin the long corn now! (financially well off)*
- *A buggy whip can't take the place of corn.*
- *Corn must be knee high by the 4th of July.*
- *Plant your corn when the leaves of the oak tree are the size of mouse's ears.[18]*

VEGETABLES

SCALLOPED TOMATOES

Butter a casserole dish and preheat oven to 350°. Layer sliced tomatoes (use sun ripened Beefsteak tomatoes if you can) with sliced onions and soft breadcrumbs. Sprinkle with fresh thyme and pepper. Cover the top with sharp cheddar cheese, then sprinkle a few breadcrumbs on top. Bake 15-20 minutes until bubbly.

Photo courtesy of Oregon State Historical Society

VEGETABLES

ETTA'S EGGS AND BAKED TOMATOES

Bet you never heard of this one! If Etta was still with us today, she might top these with grated white cheddar cheese the last 5 minutes of baking and serve them with hot pepper sauce and sprigs of fresh cilantro.

Photo courtesy Mars Hill College

"Plunge 6 medium tomatoes into boiling water and remove skins. Cut off tops and remove seeds and centers. Into each, slip from the shell one raw egg. Season with salt and pepper. Cook at 375° until the eggs are set. Serve at once."

ETTA'S BAKED CORN IN PEPPER CASES

"Cut from the cob, corn to make 1 pint. Scald 6 or 8 bullnosed peppers for 5 minutes. Rub off the skins. Cut stem end and scrape out seeds. Make a cream sauce with:

    1 Tbs. flour
    1 Tbs. butter
    1 cup thin cream (can substitute whole milk)
    1 tsp. salt

Fill peppers with corn and sauce and bake in a glass dish in a hot oven (375°) for 30 minutes."

Note: See page 69 for pepper source.

Fetching water either from the well (above) or a "headed-up" spring (right) was an ever present task...pleasant in summer, arduous in winter.

Photo courtesy Mars Hill College

VEGETABLES

BAKED APPLE-STUFFED PUMPKIN

Cut the top off a small flat, cooking pumpkin. Scrape seeds and pulp out well. Fill the pumpkin with peeled, sliced apples. Choose apples that are firm and hold their shape well when cooked (Granny Smith, Winesap). Toss the apples with a little brown sugar, cinnamon to taste, a pinch of nutmeg, then dot with a few pats of butter. Replace top and place in a baking dish. Pour about an inch of water in the dish  and place the pumpkin in a 325° oven to bake until tender (about an hour, depending on the size of the pumpkin). Serve on a platter. Diners will scoop out the cooked pumpkin along with the apples.

Note: Field pumpkins (the Cinderella type) aren't good for cooking. Small Sugar (also called New England Pie) pumpkins are favorites for baking. Look for them at tailgate and farmer's markets in the fall. For gardners, seeds are available from Burpee's (800-888-1447) and Pinetree Garden Seeds (207-926-3400).

CARROT PUFFS 1744

*This recipe comes from a delightful 18th century kitchen garden cookbook called **Adam's Luxury and Eve's Cookery.***

"Scrape and then boil your carrots; then mash them, and to a pint of pulp, grate the crumb of a penny loaf, with eggs, nutmeg, orange-flower water, and sugar to your taste. Mix all up with a little sack (sherry) and cream, and fry them in fine suet, which must be hot when you put them in your pan; a spoonful for each puff in a place."

Though not authentic, here's how I make the carrot puffs:
Peel and slice one large carrot per person served. Boil until soft, then drain and mash. Add to the pulp equal amounts of fine breadcrumbs, one egg, a little fresh grated nutmeg, a squirt of orange juice, a spoonful of sherry, a dash of sugar, and a little cream or half-and-half to bind mixture. Saute in a frying pan in a little butter until browned.

VEGETABLES

Photo courtesy Library of Congress

1883 POTATO RISSOLES

"Mash potatoes, salt and pepper to taste; if desired add a little parsley. Roll the potatoes into small balls, dip them in egg and then bread-crumbs, and fry in a bit of butter in an iron skillet." You can also bake them in a hot (400°) oven until browned. Just drizzle a little butter or some grated cheese over them first.[4]

Onion Weather Forecast

Onion's skin very thin, mild winter's coming in;
Onion's skin thick and rough, coming winter cold and rough.[20]

VEGETABLES

Photo courtesy of University of Louisville, Kentucky

Perhaps the pan on the back of the stove is full of simmering green beans. Notice the shuck beans hanging to dry behind the stove. When dry, this cook will remove the strings and store the beans in a burlap sack.

1891 Advice to the Harried
When you are tired of life, and all its busy scenes.
Just jump into the garden, and hide behind the beans![19]

VEGETABLES

1908 ONIONS STUFFED WITH NUTS

"Cook eight onions until nearly tender then cut out the centers to form cases. Fill with one cup bread crumbs, ½ cup chopped nut meats, 2 Tbs. melted butter, ¼ tsp. each salt and pepper. Cook in a baking dish, surrounded with hot broth or water until done. Serve with or without cream sauce."[6]

GELEMA'S POT OF GREEN BEANS

"First," says Gelema Worley of Big Pine, N.C., "you have to grow the best bean, which is a Cornfield bean." These are meaty pole beans with seeds that are big when they're ready to pick. Then you string them and snap them between each seed. Put them in a pot of boiling water and parboil them for a few minutes. Pour the water out, and add fresh water to cover along with a piece of "middlin meat" (meat streaked salt pork). You can use ham or browned bacon if you like. Simmer for 2-3 hours. You want the liquid to cook down, but don't let it disappear. Salt and pepper to taste.

SHUCK BEANS

Shuck beans, also called Leather Britches, are dried green beans. Gelema says she doesn't eat them until there's snow on the ground (which would be November in the North Carolina mountains). To make them, pick, string, and snap good pole beans as above. Then run a string through them and hang them to dry in a warm place (see photo left). Gelema spreads them out on paper in a warm upstairs room to dry instead of stringing. You can store them in jars, or bag them in burlap or a cotton feed sack like in the old days. To prepare the beans, rinse, parboil, and rinse again. Then slow cook with ham, bacon, or salt pork for several hours until done.

APPLES & BERRIES

OLD FASHIONED APPLESAUCE DUMPLINGS

2 cups applesauce   ½ tsp. cinnamon
¼ cup brown sugar   ½ cup water
½ recipe biscuit dough (see page 18)

Combine the first four ingredients and gently simmer on medium-low heat in a lidded pan. Drop dumpling dough by spoonfuls onto top of simmering sauce. Cover and cook for 10 minutes. If you have the heat up too high, the sauce will burn. Slide fruit and dumplings into a bowl and sprinkle top with cinnamon sugar. Serve as a side dish with pork, chicken, or duck.

Photo courtesy of Alice Lloyd College, Ky.

The woman in this picture could be making applesauce dumplings from summer apples. She's made a washpan of biscuits, and she's stirring something on her wood cook stove. Note the corn growing just outside the kitchen door. This family is farming every speck of space that's available to them.

APPLES & BERRIES

MOM'S APPLE COBBLER

Effie Price's mother, Emma, used to bake this tasty cobbler in her Home Comfort cook stove when Effie was growing up in the N.C. mountains.

1½ cups self-rising flour
½ cup shortening
One third cup milk
3 finely chopped apples

½ cup butter
2 cups sugar
2 cups water
1 tsp. cinnamon

Heat oven to 350°. Melt ½ cup butter in a 9x13 inch baking dish. In a saucepan, heat sugar and water until dissolved. Cut shortening into flour to make fine particles, add milk, and stir with a fork only until dough leaves the side of the bowl. Turn out onto a pastry cloth and knead until smooth. Divide dough into two balls. Roll each ball of dough into a large rectangle ¼ inch thick. Sprinkle cinnamon on apples and spread over dough. Roll up jelly roll style and place in the pan of melted butter. Pour sugar syrup carefully around rolls. Bake one hour.

White Mountain apple peeler, 1880s

EASY APPLE DUMPLING PIE

Peel and core one tart cooking apple per person and place in the bottom of a buttered glass dish. Pour in ½ cup water. Make or buy a pie crust and lay over the apples. Turn under pastry edges and flute between finger and thumb. Cut a hole in the pastry that exposes the center of each apple (the inside hole of a donut cutter works well.) Put into each apple a teaspoon of brown sugar, pinch of cinnamon, and a tiny piece of butter. Bake in a 350° oven about 45 minutes until crust is brown and juices are bubbly.

Photo courtesy of Mars Hill College

APPLES & BERRIES

Photo courtesy Library of Congress

BOILED CIDER FRUIT CAKE

From a 1932 newspaper scrap found in Aunt Jane's Cookbook.

Cook together rather slowly until boiling point is reached:
>1 cup sweet cider
>1 cup brown sugar
>1 cup raisins or dates (or both)
>½ cup butter

Remove from the fire when the mixture boils, and have ready:
>2 cups flour sifted with:
>>½ tsp. salt
>>2 tsp. baking powder
>>1 tsp. baking soda
>>1 tsp. cinnamon
>>½ tsp. each of ginger and grated nutmeg

Add this mixture, not by degrees, but all at once. Stir rapidly into the hot ingredients without a moment's delay after these have been removed from the fire. Bake in a greased tube pan in a moderate oven (350º) for 30 minutes or until firm.

Apples & Berries

Etta's Strawberry Dumplings, 1916

Make a recipe of biscuit dough (pg. 18), adding two tablespoons of white sugar to the mixture.

Roll the dough out into a one third inch-thick rectangle. Cut into six squares. Cover each square with sliced, fresh strawberries that have been tossed with a little sugar. Draw the edges of the dough up over fruit and pinch together at the top if you can. If dough doesn't meet at the top, just leave open. Place dumplings onto a greased baking pan. Brush the tops with butter and sprinkle with sugar. Bake in a hot (375°) oven about 15 minutes until nicely browned. Etta served these with a "thick sauce" that was probably made from butter, vanilla, powdered sugar, and milk or bourbon.

Photo courtesy Colorado Historical Society

Making butter with a side crank barrel churn.

APPLES & BERRIES

JEWEL BERRY FOOL

Vintage advertising cookbooks are fun to collect. They reveal a glimpse of life in days gone by. This recipe comes from a Jewel shortening cookbook published in the late 1930s.

> 2 cups pitted cherries, raspberries, gooseberries,
> blackberries, strawberries, or blueberries
> ½ cup butter
> 1½ cups sugar
> 2 eggs

Fill a Jewel pastry-lined pie plate with berries. Beat together butter and sugar, then eggs. Spread over berries. Bake in a 450° oven for 10 minutes. Reduce heat to 325° and bake 30 minutes. Serve hot.[15]

Photo courtesty Library of Congress

"Making biscuits for dinner on corn shucking day, 1939." Notice the stack cake on the table and the tin of Jewel shortening on the shelf next to the flowers.

DESSERTS

LITTLE GINGER NUTS, 1906

½ cup white sugar
1 cup molasses
½ cup melted butter
1 egg, well beaten
3½ cups flour

½ tsp. salt
½ tsp. cloves
1 tsp. cinnamon
2 tsp. ground ginger
1 tsp. soda

Mix soda in a little boiling water; stir into molasses. Add the butter, egg, salt, and spices, part of flour then the sugar, then the remainder of flour. When well beaten together, flour the hands and take off pieces the size of large nutmegs; roll lightly. Roll each in granulated sugar, and place one inch apart in pans and bake in quick oven. (A quick oven would be about 375°).[6]

AUNT MAGGIE'S SPICED JINI CAKES

Aunt Maggie was the backyard neighbor of my grandparents, Maudie and Emery Smith. They lived in the small town of Salem, West Virginia. Though Aunt Maggie has long since passed, her unusual cookie recipe lives on in my grandmother's tattered, yellowed, food stained, hand-written cookbook.

2 cups sugar
1 cup shortening
2 eggs
1 cup coconut
1 tsp. each of soda, cocoa, cinnamon, and vanilla

2 cups chopped apples
3 cups flour
½ cup cold coffee
½ tsp. salt, cloves, nutmeg

Beat sugar, shortening, eggs, and vanilla until fluffy. Sift dry ingredients and add to creamed mixture alternately with coffee. Stir in coconut and apples. Drop by spoonful onto greased cookie sheet and bake at 350° until done. (If you don't like coffee, you can substitute milk, buttermilk, or sour cream).

DESSERTS

JOHNNIE'S SALTY PEANUT COOKIES

Johnnie Cole Otto was born and raised in the Great Smoky Mountains National Park before it became a park in the 1930s. She recently passed away, but her fabulous Southern Mountain cooking and her stories of growing up as a pioneer child into a strong and spunky woman touched my life and the lives of countless others.

1 cup shortening	1 tsp. baking powder
2 cups brown sugar	1 tsp. soda
2 eggs	2 cups oats
2 ¼ cups flour	2 cups crisp rice cereal
1 cup salted peanuts	1 tsp. vanilla

Cream shortening and sugar. Beat in eggs, baking powder, soda, and vanilla until well combined. Blend in flour. Chop peanuts and stir into mixture along with the oats and rice cereal. Refrigerate for one hour, then drop by spoonfuls onto greased cookie sheet and bake in a 350° oven 15 minutes or until lightly browned.

Photo by Richard Renfro

The Cole cabin, where Johnnie Otto and her 12 siblings grew up. It can be visited in the Great Smoky Mountains National Park on the Roaring Fork Auto Tour near Gatlinburg, Tennessee.

DESSERTS

ALL TO THE GOOD GINGERBREAD, 1910

½ cup sugar
½ cup molasses
1 egg
¼ cup butter
1½ cup pastry flour

½ cup buttermilk
1 tsp. soda (dissolve in milk)
1 tsp. ginger
½ tsp. cinnamon

Cream sugar, molasses, and butter. Beat in egg. Mix spices with the flour and add alternately with the buttermilk and soda. Pour into a buttered glass dish or iron skillet. Bake at 350° for 25-35 minutes or until cake springs back to a light touch.[6]

Photo courtesy Great Smoky Mtns. Nat. Park

"Boiling the syrup" to make sorghum molasses in Tennessee, 1927

QUICK FRUIT UPSIDE-DOWN GINGERBREAD

We cook this frequently at our log cabin in the wood cook stove. Using canned pie filling is cheating...but if you're cooking by lantern light, like we do, or if you're camping, no one will mind!

Butter your iron skillet or dutch oven and add a can of apple, cherry, peach, or blackberry pie filling, spreading it out evenly. (We've tried every fruit and prefer apple). Pour the gingerbread batter on top of the fruit and bake about 25 minutes in a 350° oven until the cake is done. If you're camping and using a size 8 dutch oven, put some coals underneath and just a few on top of your pan. Check after 20 minutes. To serve, spoon out and top with freshly whipped cream.

DESERTS

NITA'S COCONUT STACK CAKE

Nita says, "This recipe is way over 100 years old, and if you don't like this cake, something's wrong!" When she was a child growing up on her parent's farm in Charlotte, N.C., her neighbor, Mamie Orr, used to make this cake. Nita remembers Mamie standing in her kitchen cooking a turkey, making vegetables, preparing cornbread, and stirring this cake on her hip all at the same time.

2 cups sugar
1 cup butter
1 cup milk
3 or 4 eggs

3 cups flour
1 Tbs. vanilla
2 tsp. baking powder
Coconut (bagged or fresh)

Cream sugar and butter until fluffy. Beat in eggs one at a time. Mix in vanilla, baking powder, and a handful of coconut. Add flour alternately with milk until batter is smooth. Pour into 3 buttered cake pans, and bake in a preheated 350° oven until lightly browned.

Cake Filling:
Combine in a saucepan: whites of two eggs, 2 Tbs. flour, 1½ cup sugar, ½ tsp. salt, butter the size of an egg, and "as much coconut as you like." Cook until thick. Cool a bit, then spread on cake layers. Finish with a thin layer of filling on top, and sprinkle with grated coconut.

Nita's father-in-law built her beautiful home in 1900. The house faces an incredible view of the French Broad River meandering through a secluded Western North Carolina mountain valley.

LOVE

BEWARE, OH, BEWARE

West Virginia fiddler Blind Alfred Reed recorded this version of an 1860s folksong in 1929. He penned and sang songs that reflected social controversies of the time such as "Why Do You Bob Your Hair, Girls?" in reaction to the flappers, as well as this entertaining song that served as a warning to women about associating with reckless men.

We know young men are bold and free; beware, oh, take care,
They tell you they're friends but they're liars you see, beware, oh take care.

Chorus:
Beware young ladies they're fooling you,
Trust them not, they're fooling you,
Beware young ladies, they're fooling you,
Beware, oh, take care.

They smoke, they chew, they wear fine shoes, beware, oh take care;
And in their pocket is a bottle of booze, beware, oh take care.

Around their neck they wear a guard, beware, oh take care;
And in their pocket is a deck of cards, beware, oh take care.

They put their hands up to their hearts, they sigh, oh they sigh;
They say they love no one but you, they lie, oh they lie!

Nita's Romantic Advice

When Nita Stackhouse became interested in boys around 1920, her father, James Caldwell, used to tell her:

    **"Don't even go with anybody you can't marry,
    because you don't know who you're gonna love."**

Nita and Gilbert Stackhouse were happily married for 58 years, and speaking of him still lights her face. So I asked her, "What's your secret to a long and wonderful marriage?" Nita told me, "People think they're in love, when they only like each other. They marry before they find real love, because they don't know any better. I was lucky that I waited until I found my true love and I married him."

DESSERTS

GELEMA'S APPLE STACK CAKE

If you mention Apple Stack Cake to anyone in Big Pine Valley, N.C., they're going to tell you that Gelema Worley makes the best. And if you're lucky, you'll have the winning bid for the one she makes for the annual local fire department auction. Legend has it that in years past, pioneer brides of little means would ask each guest to bring a layer for the cake on her wedding day. The bride's mother would make the applesauce and stack the cake. If the bride had lots of friends, she'd have a real tall cake.

1¼ cups milk	1 tsp. vanilla
1¼ cup sugar	2 big Tbs. shortening
2 eggs	Self rising flour
Apples (about 10)	
Big pinch each of cinnamon, ginger, and cloves	

Beat shortening, sugar, and eggs until fluffy. Add vanilla and spices and combine well. Pour in milk, stir, then add enough flour to make a dough that's as stiff as cake mix batter. Preheat your oven to about 300°, and divide batter into 4 greased cake pans. Bake until lightly browned.

FILLING (MAKE BEFORE CAKES)

Make a thick applesauce and spread on warm cakes.

Gelema told me this as though anyone could whip up a delicious applesauce like she makes. Knowing that everybody thinks hers is special, I coaxed these secrets from her: She uses Johathan, Grimes Golden or Striped apples, peels and slices them, sprinkles sugar on them and lets them "set" until they get juicy. Then Gelema puts the apples in a pan, adds some cinnamon, and slowly cooks them until they're soft, stirring until the lumps are mostly gone. Don't add water unless they're sticking. She doesn't add any; that's why the flavor is so intense. Cool the applesauce to room temperature, then spread on warm cakes, stacking as you go, finishing with a layer of sauce on the top. Store in an airtight container. The cake improves with age, not that it will get a chance to!

DESSERTS

JAM PIE

2 eggs, separated	1½ tsp. flour
½ cup sugar	Pinch nutmeg and allspice
½ cup homemade jam	1 unbaked pie shell
½ cup cream	¼ tsp. cream of tartar
½ Tbs. butter, softened	¼ cup sugar

Beat egg yolks with ½ cup sugar, jam, cream, butter, flour, and spices. Pour into pie shell. Bake at 300 ° for 45-60 minutes until set. Beat egg whites until they stand in stiff peaks. Gradually add cream of tartar and ¼ sugar. Pile on top of pie and bake about 15 minutes at 375° until meringue is lightly browned.[12]

Pie Eating Contest, 1945   Photo courtesy of Denver Public Library

---

Cake Lore

•*Always bake a cake while the sun is going up (or it will fall.)*
•*Don't throw away the egg shells until after the cake is baked.*
•*Stop the clock while the cake is baking.*[18]

DESSERTS

Photo courtesy of Library of Congress

DESSERTS

CHOCOLATE POP-CORN

From a 1914 newspaper clipping found in Etta's hand-written cookbook.

1 quart popped corn	½ cup milk
1 cup granulated sugar	3 Tbs. grated chocolate
Butter the size of a walnut	

"This is one of the simpliest of all confections to prepare, but it ranks with the best as to quality. The corn should be freshly popped. The other ingredients should be cooked together until a little of it dropped into cold water is quite brittle. Pour it over the corn, stirring so that all the kernels are coated. Eat while still fresh and before the crispness is gone from the candy."

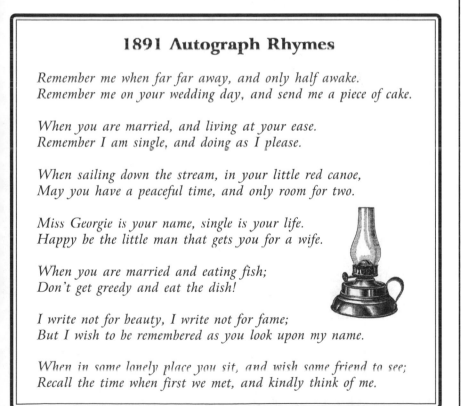

1891 Autograph Rhymes

Remember me when far far away, and only half awake.
Remember me on your wedding day, and send me a piece of cake.

When you are married, and living at your ease.
Remember I am single, and doing as I please.

When sailing down the stream, in your little red canoe,
May you have a peaceful time, and only room for two.

Miss Georgie is your name, single is your life.
Happy be the little man that gets you for a wife.

When you are married and eating fish;
Don't get greedy and eat the dish!

I write not for beauty, I write not for fame;
But I wish to be remembered as you look upon my name.

When in some lonely place you sit, and wish some friend to see;
Recall the time when first we met, and kindly think of me.

Pickles & Butters

Pickling was especially important as a method of preserving the summer harvest in the days before refrigeration. Cabbage, green beans, onions, peppers, corn, and cucumbers were among the many vegetables that could be found sitting in salt brines in ceramic crocks in pioneer root cellars.

Effie pictured in front of a crazy quilt that she and fellow quilting guild members created for a community fundraising event.

The women who shared their recipes for this book lived without refrigeration (or electricity) until they were adults. And though they don't have to grow and put up their food now, they still keep their cellar houses filled with preserved treasures from their gardens. After all, you just can't buy pickled cornfield beans at the store! When we open a jar of Effie Price's pickles or her sweet, creamy apple butter at our house, the contents are all but gone in minutes. The recipes that follow are Effie's.

Refrigerator Pickles

Slice enough cukes and onions to make a gallon. Effie uses small pickling cucumbers that she grows in her garden. Pack cucumbers into glass jars.

In a saucepan, combine:
1¾ cups sugar
2 tsp. salt (pickling or non-iodized)
1 cup white vinegar
1 tsp. celery seed

Heat until sugar melts. Cool and pour over the cucumbers. Put lids on the jars, but don't seal. Refrigerate. These will keep about 4 months in your refrigerator or 10 minutes in ours.

Summer Complaint

At summer's end I am a wreck from canning foodstuffs by the peck,
But I stagger back with sticky pride and bless the bottles, side by side,
Of apples, plums, and succotash and beans, and peas, as good as cash.
Now all I need is a recipe for canning and preserving ME! [7]

PICKLES & BUTTERS

Mr. Tag to Miss Pickle, 1832

My heart to rags with love is torn, and scratch'd with doubts hard to be borne.
My soul is harrow'd up with grief, till naught but Pickle gives relief.
> *Not pickled onions, 'tis I mean;*
> *Nor pickled cabbage, red or green;*
> *Nor pickled cucumbers, small or big;*
> *Nor pickled pork, nor pickled pig;*
> *Not pickles brought from foreign shore,*
> *Nor any pickle known before!*
A pickle, ad infinitum bright, 'tis brightest day 'midst darkest night!
A pickle 'tis of virgin fame, and Bridget Pickle is its name.
Oh! then, kind Cupid, be not fickle; inspire the heart of sweet Miss Pickle
To reap love's harvest with thy sickle; Oh! Pickle! Pickle! Pickle! Pickle![22]

Does He Love Me?

When Effie was a girl, she and her girl-friends would predict their future love lives by consulting the love-vine, which grows abundantly in the North Carolina mountains. According to Effie, here's how it works:

> *"First, you name the boy that you like. Then you take one of the long orange tendrils off the plant and try to tie it in a knot, which is most difficult. If you can tie a knot in the vine without breaking it, then the boy you named loves you."*

Plant or Beast?

Love-vine is commonly known as Dodder, and is less affectionately referred to as Strangle-weed, Devil's Hair, and Hell-bind due to its parasitic nature. The long, orange, thread-like stems, while being useful for de-termining your romantic future, also spread quickly over host plants, drawing the life from them with sucking organs.

Pickles & Butters

Old-Timey Pickled Beans

Snap Half Runner or Cornfield beans. Cook until you can mash a bean between your fingers. Drain and let cool. Layer beans with salt in a 4 gallon crock (a layer of beans, a layer of salt, and so on). Pour warm spring water over beans to cover. Put a plate on top, a rock on top of that, and tie a cloth over all. Watch to see that the water runs over the beans (that's a good thing; it means they're fermenting). They should be ready to can or eat in 9 or 10 days. Wash salt out before eating.

Photo courtesy Mars Hill College

Fast Pickled Beans

Snap, cook, cool, and drain beans as above. Let them "set" until completely cold. Drain and pack into jars. Meanwhile, combine one gallon warm water with one cup white vinegar and one cup salt. Pour over beans. Put lids on tight. Let ferment for a week, then refrigerate or can.

Secrets:
• *Choose a green bean variety with a big bean like Half Runners.*
• *Snap your beans between each bean seed. Don't cut with a knife.*

PICKLES & BUTTERS

EFFIE'S APPLE BUTTER

Fill a 6 quart pan with peeled, cored, sliced apples. Effie combines different varieties, depending on what she has on hand. Add enough water to keep apples from sticking as they cook. (The SECRET is to add almost no water, and constantly stir your apples on low heat until they're cooked). When the apples are cooked, take a potato masher to them until no lumps remain. Add:

2 tsp. cinnamon	2-3 cups sugar (personal preference)
½ tsp. cloves	¼ cup lemon juice
½ tsp. allspice	¼ cup vinegar

Pour into a crock pot and cook 2-4 hours (or more) on low. You can can the hot apple butter or pour cooled sauce into jars and refrigerate for about three weeks.

Note: If you can, buy locally grown cooking apples at your local farmer's market. They have so much more flavor than most cold-stored commercial varieties.

"Preserving"　　　　　　　　*Photo courtesy Library of Congress*

THE CELLAR HOUSE

Cellar houses were (and still are) built into a hillside, with the exposed portions made of rock. Food could be protected from freezing in harsh winters and spoiling in the summer heat. Bins for potatoes could be found against one wall while bushel baskets of apples and root vegetables would be found in another corner. Crocks of pickled vegetables such as beans, cukes, sauerkraut, or corn were to be found under the shelves that lined the walls clear up to the ceiling. The shelves were carefully filled with every kind of canned fruits and vegetables you could imagine.

TO CURE EGGS, 1900

Chickens that live outside in cool climates don't do much egg laying during the winter months. Here's one way of making sure you don't run out of eggs this winter:

"Slack a lump of lime as large as a man's hat crown in 2 gallons of water, let it settle and pour off, then add a large handful of salt. Put any number of eggs this will cover in a stone jar, water, and put in a cold, dark place. They may be put down in the 5th month (May), and they are good all winter. This gives plenty of eggs for cooking, when fresh ones cannot be had." From the Women's Auxiliary of Chester Co. Hospital

Photo by Wayne Erbsen

Ray Worley and his father built the cellar house (pictured above) in 1940 along with the farmhouse where he and his wife, Margaret, live in the North Carolina mountains.

Ray stands inside the cellar with a few of the many canned vegetables and fruits that Margaret and he put up from their garden each summer.

MOCK FOODS

M ock recipes are the hallmark of the innovative, spunky cook. If you could step back in time and peek at the creator of a mock recipe, you'd likely find that the author was not about to let scarcity get in the way of her good cooking. Mock cooking was especially popular among those who were used to having a variety of ingredients available for their use in cooking, but now found themselves far from familiar surroundings. Colonial American settlers substituted corn meal (called Indian meal) for wheat flour, and pioneer lemonade consisted of water, vinegar, and molasses.

The Great Depression found most American cooks in want of anything that couldn't be grown or picked. Cookbooks of the 1930s and 40s are full of mock recipes. Some of the recipes that follow sound pretty disgusting (Mock Turtle Soup); others are good and worth trying, especially the Mock Macaroons.

Photo courtesy Florida State Archives

MOCK CHERRY PIE

1 cup halved cranberries	1½ cups cold water
1 cup raisins	1 Tbs. cornstarch
1 cup sugar	

Add cornstarch to cold water. Stir to dissolve. Add remaining ingredients and cook until mixture thickens. Pour cooled mixture into a pie plate lined with pastry. Cover with top crust and bake at 350° until browned and bubbly.[4]

Mock Foods

Mock Turtle Soup, 1933

"Let someone besides yourself clean a calf-head, removing brains and tongue whole, the meat from the bone, and chopping the bone into several pieces; put all to soak separately in salt-water for several minutes to bleach; use brain and tongue for separate dishes, turning meat and bone into soup..."

The lengthy recipe then recommends that the tongue be boiled with parsley, celery, bay leaf, cloves, cinnamon, allspice, carrot, and turnip, along with the head meat. You take out the tongue to serve on it's own, then make two different stocks from veal and the calf head bones. One wonders if it wouldn't be easier to start with a turtle![16]

Etta's Mock Honey, 1906

"One pound sugar, one orange, four eggs well beaten, ¼ pound butter, juice of two lemons, grated rind of one lemon. Stir over a fire until smooth. Try this."

Mock Macaroni, 1824

Break some crackers in small pieces, soak them in milk until they are soft; then use them as a substitute for macaroni.[13]

Mock Coconut Macaroons

½ cup softened butter	1 tsp. baking powder
1 cup sugar	½ tsp. salt
2 egg whites	¼ cup flour
¾ tsp. almond extract	2½ cups rolled oats

Beat shortening, sugar, and egg whites until fluffy. Add extract, baking powder, salt, and flour and continue to beat until well combined. Stir in (do not beat) oats. Drop by spoonful onto ungreased cookie sheet and bake at 350° until lightly browned.[6]

CHORES

NOW-A-DAYS

Alas! how everything has changed
Since I was sweet sixteen,
When all the girls wore home-spun gowns,
And aprons nice and clean;
With bonnets made of braided straw,
That tied beneath the chin,
And shawls laid neatly on the neck,
That fastened with a pin.

Photo courtesy Mars Hill College

But now-a-days the ladies wear
French gloves and large bonnets,
That take up full, a yard of sky, in coal hod shape or flats;
With gowns the sleeves like bags they flow, their arms not seen at all,
With waists that you might break in two, they are so very small.

I recollect the time when I rode father's horse to mill,
Across the meadow, wood, and field, and up and down the hill.
And when our folks were out at work; as true as I'm a sinner,
I jump'd upon a horse, bare-back, and carried them their dinner.

Dear me! Young ladies now-a-days would almost faint away,
To think of riding all alone, in wagon, chaise or sleigh.
And as for giving Pa his meals, or helping Ma to bake,
Oh, saints! twould spoil their lily hands, though sometimes they make cake.

When winter came, the maiden's heart
Began to beat and flutter;
Each beau would take his sweetheart out,
Sleigh riding in a cutter.
Or if the storm was bleak and cold,
The girls and beaux together
Would meet and have most glorious fun,
And never mind the weather.

But now-a-days, it grieves me much,
The circumstance to mention,
However kind a young man's heart,
And honest his intention,
He ne'er can ask a girl to ride, but such a war is waged!
And if he sees her once a week, why surely they're engaged!

The Old Farmer's Almanack, 1832

CHORES

If you think you're too tired to cook dinner, then consider a day in the life of Effie Price, whose log cabin we bought in a remote mountain cove in the Big Pine section of Madison County, N.C. Here, she tells of a typical day as a 14 year-old in 1928:

"I got up at 5:00 a.m. to feed the hogs and chickens and gather the eggs by lantern-light. Then I helped my mother cook breakfast (in the wood cook stove). After eating, Mommy would wash the dishes while my brother Dewey and I milked the cows and put the milk in the spring box to cool. In spring, summer, and fall we'd all go to the field with Poppy and work 'til dinner. We'd plant and hoe corn, dig 'taters (sweet and white), and tend the tobacco. We grew wheat and vegetables, too. After dinner

N.C. Archives and History

and a ten minute rest, we'd return to the fields and work 'til dark. Then it was time to milk the cows again by lantern-light. At night, we'd have a little supper, then quilt or sew before going to bed.

Saturday was "washin' day." We'd build a fire under the big iron pot that hung in the yard and haul water from the spring to heat. When the clothes dried we'd iron them with irons kept hot by the fire. Then we'd sweep the house and yard (back then, folks didn't plant grass in their yards like they do now.) Sundays, we'd hitch up the horses to the wagon and give a ride to whomever we came across walking down the road to the Baptist church. If it was a school day, chores were done before and after school.

Effie plays on the radio, 1932

Life wasn't all work. If it snowed, Dewey and I would take our guitars and head over the mountain to play music at my Uncle's house

CHORES

in Spring Creek. In the fall, we'd have bean shellings, quilting bees, and corn husking parties. The first person to find a red ear of corn would get $5.00.

My mother sewed all our clothes from cloth she bought on her monthly outing to Marshall, the nearest town. As a kid I tried sewing, but my mother thought I'd tear up the machine running it backwards and didn't want me to mess with it. So when she'd go to town, I'd have Dewey be lookout, and I learned to sew on my own. I stashed fabric under the bed, and one day I took out a pretty dress I'd sewed and sure surprised my mother. I sewed my first quilt at 13, made of feed sacks. The quilt I sleep under now is one my mother made from smoking tobacco sacks. She'd keep some white, and dye some red, then sew them up. We made all our own sheets; we'd embroider the edges at night.

Photo courtesy NC Dept. Archives & History

Dying wool

Those were the good days. I was happy as a lark. We all were. Life was simpler then; you just worked hard and slept sound. We all got along and worked together. I don't even remember being tired. I wouldn't trade those days for anything in the world!"

Photo courtesy of Georgia Department of Archives and History

Blinky Milk

Milk turning sour creates eye-bubbles. When the bubbles start winking at you it's time to churn.[18]

CHORES

GRANDMOTHER'S WEST VIRGINIA RECEET

1. Bild fire in back yard to het kettle of rain water.
2. Set tubs so smoke won't blow in eyes if wind is peart.
3. Shave 1 hold cake lie sope in biling water.
4. Sort things. Makes 3 piles. 1 pile white. 1 pile currlord. 1 pile work britches and rags.
5. Stur flour in cold water to smooth, thin down with biling water.
6. Rub dirty spots on board. Scrub hard. Then bile. Rub cullord, but don't bile, just rench and starch.
7. Take white things out of kettle with broom stick handel then rench, blew and starch.
8. Spread tee towels on grass.
9. Hang old rags on fence.
10. Pore rench water in flower bed
11. Scrub porch with soapy water.
12. Turn tubs up an dress-smooth hair with side combs. Brew cup of tee, set and rest and rock a spell and count blessins.[7]

Submitted by the Harrison County Homemakers
for the 1976 W. Va. Heritage Cookbook

Photo courtesy of Berea College, Kentucky

WEATHER LORE

- Better to be bitten by a snake than to feel the sun in March.
- The sun is none the worse for shining on a dung hill.
- It will be a clear day if everything has been eaten from supper.
- The dirt bird sings and we shall have rain.[18]

Isn't She Lovely?

Long in her sides, bright in her eyes, short in her legs, thin in her thighs,
Big in her ribs, wide in her pins, full in her bosom, small in her shins,
Long in her face, fine in her tail and never deficient in filling a pail!

Description of a good cow, 1832 Farmer's Almanack

Photo courtesy of Library of Congress

Cow Weather Forecast

A cow with its tail to the west makes weather the best;
A cow with its tail to the east makes weather the least.

You can expect rain if a cow kicks backward in the morning while being milked.

When cows don't give milk, expect stormy and cold weather.[18]

FOLK REMEDIES

"Sowing for Diptheria"   *Harper's Weekly, January 15, 1881*

Diptheria was a much feared and misunderstood disease at the time this drawing was published. The bacteria was spread by coughing or sneezing, not via contaminated water as indicated above. Victims (most often children) succumbed to death in 50% of cases because of the thick membrane that covered the throat and the toxins produced by the bacteria. Frequently, several family members died within days of each other due to the brief 1-4 day incubation period. Fortunately, an antioxin for the widespread disease became available in 1895, paving the way for the immunization which has made Diptheria a rare disease in America today.

Folk Remedies

E ven though medical advances like immunizations and the germ theory improved the lives of Americans by 1900, patent medicines and folk remedies were still popular, especially in rural, isolated communities. The remedies and superstitions on the following pages were collected up through the 1950's and are offered for your entertainment only!

Uses for Rattlesnake Oil

CORNS: Apply rattlesnake or mud turtle oil to corns before bedtime for several nights.
CROUP: Rub rattlesnake oil on the outside of the throat and a few drops in the mouth.
DEAFNESS: A drop in the affected ear once a day.
DIPTHERIA: ¼ tsp. every hour.

Bat Lore

- *If a bat bites you, your ears and nose will change places.*
- *If a bat runs into your head, you'll soon become baldheaded.*
- *Bat blood is a cure for baldness.*[18]

Old-Timey Miseries:

Chilblain, ague, cow itch, dew sores, dropsy, falling palate, plat-eye, phthisic, quinsy, snow blindness, train sickness, wens, morbis, biliousness.

Autograph Rhymes, 1896

- *When you get old and cannot see, put on your specks and look at me.*
- *Life is short. O may it be, full of happiness for thee.*[19]

Folk Remedies

TO PREVENT LOCKJAW if a needle is stuck in the foot, put fat meat next to the puncture and a penny over that.

TO CURE A FEVER BLISTER, kiss a red-headed man.[18]

A GOOD SPRING TONIC is anvil dust mixed with cream.

TOASTED EGG-SHELL TEA is good for what ails you.

TO CURE ASTHMA, stick the dried skin of a mole to the chest with honey.

TO PREVENT MUMPS, cut a chip off an old log trough, carry it in your pocket, and rub it on your jaws and throat every day.

TO PREVENT A COLD, tie a big red onion to the bedpost.[21]

Harpers Weekly 1/15/1881

"How to dispose of sewerage", 1881

CURE FOR BALDNESS: Consume the gall of a lizard, fresh mouse meat or mole's blood.

FALLEN PALATE: A lock of hair tied tightly at the top of the head will pull up a fallen palate.

CURE FOR FEVER: *Seed of parsley, dill, and rue*
Of Celandine and feverfew;
Take equal parts of all these worts,
And you'll be ready for any sport.[18]

HAIR LORE

HAIR RHYMES

- Comb your hair in the dark, comb your sorrows to your heart. Comb your hair in the day, comb your sorrows far away.
- Friday cut and Sunday shorn, better to never have been born.
- Chicken in the house, rooster on the fence. Johnny get your hair cut, fifteen cents.[18]

Photo courtesy of Florida State Archives

IT'S BAD LUCK TO:

Comb your hair after supper, find one of your hairs in a bird's nest, burn your own hair, drop a comb while combing, cut your hair when you're sick, or place a hat on a bed.

Women and Shaving

In the mid 1700s, women shaved their foreheads and eyebrows so they could wear press-on mouse skin eyebrows.

American women started shaving in 1915 following a popular advertisement of a woman with shaved armpits.

NOTES

It's good luck to share your seeds,
but it's bad luck to thank anyone for seeds or plants.

Photo courtesy Great Smoky Mountains National Park

RESOURCES

Acanthus Books
www.acanthus-books.com
Large selection of culinary and household history books.

Bibliofind
www.bibliofind.com
Locates out-of-print, rare, and antiquarian books.

Food Heritage Press
www.foodbooks.com
Great selection of historic cookbooks, both in and out-of-print.

The Amish Country Store
(727) 587-9657
www.theamishcountrystore.com
Copes dried sweet corn, shoofly pie mix, gifts.

DL Landreth Seed Co.
(800) 654-2407
They sell Bull Nose Pepper seeds, and other heirloom seeds.

RH Shumway's Seeds
(803) 663-9771
www.rhshumway.com
Cornfield beans and other heirloom seeds, great old-timey catalogue.

Great Smoky Mountains Natural History Association
(865) 436-0120   Fax (865) 436-6884
Best whole wheat flour there is, worth every cent of shipping costs.

Big Spring Mill,
Virginia's Best Self-Rising Flour and other flours
Elliston, Va. 24087
Wonderful biscuit flour. They'll mail from their 150 yr. old mill.

Old Mill of Guilford
(336) 643-4783
1340 NC 68, North Oak Ridge, N.C. 27310
Stone ground flours and delicious imaginative mixes for baked goods.

CREDITS

COOKBOOKS

1. *Adam's Luxury and Eve's Cookery, 1746*, Facimile Ed. Prospect Books, 1983
2. Applied Arts Publishers, *The Lancaster County Farm Cook Book*, 1967
3. Bryan, Lettice, *The Kentucky Housewife, 1839*. Reprint Image Graphics
4. Buckeye Publishing Co., *Practical Housekeeping*, 1883
5. Calumet Baking Company, *Reliable Recipes*, no date...probably 1930s.
6. *Etta's Handwritten Recipe Notebook*, 1906-1918
7. Harrison County Extension Homemakers, *West Virginia Heritage Recipes*, 1976
8. Kander, Mrs. Simon, *The Settlement Cook Book*, 1915
9. Kerr *Home Canning Cookbook*, 1934
10. Leslie, Eliza, *The Indian Meal Book*, 1846, Reprint by Lawrence Burns, 1998
11. *Majestic Range Cook Book*, Majestic Manufacturing Company, about 1910
12. Malone, Ruth & Lankford, Bess, *The Arkansas Classic Cookbook*, 1993
13. Randolph, Mary, *The Virginia House-wife,1824*, Fascimile Univ. S.C. Press, 1984
14. Rorer, Sarah Tyson, *Snowdrift Shortening Secrets*, 1913
15. Tested Recipes with Jewel Shortening: *The Choice of Good Cooks*, 1930s
16. Wrought Iron Range Co., *The Home Comfort Cook Book*, 1933

FOLKLORE

17. Boatright, Hudson, and Maxwell, *Texas Folk and Folklore*, 1954
18. Brown, Frank C., *North Carolina Folklore*, Volumes 1, 6, 7, 1964
19. *Georgetta's Autograph Album* 1891-1896
20. Kingsbury, Stewart and Mildred, *Weather Wisdom*, 1996.
21. Randolph, Vance, *Ozark Superstitions*, 1946
22. The Old Farmer's Almanack, 1832
23. Thomas, Daniel & Lucy, *Kentucky Superstitions*, 1920

THANKS!

To Effie Price, Margaret and Ray Worley, Gelema Worley, and Juanita Stackhouse for sharing recipes, stories, and wisdom. Steve Millard, cover design and graphic arts; Jimmy Greene (A&J Trade Cards) for the Victorian era trade card image pictured on the cover; Will Pruett for advice on great local cooks. Marti Otto and Richard Renfro, photo researchers; Bess Lankford and Nancy Swell recipes; Janet Swell, Lori Erbsen, Beverly Teeman, Bonnie Neustein, David Currier, Jennifer Thomas, editing. Leon Swell computer support. Taste testers included Annie, Wes, Rita, & Wayne Erbsen, Elaine Craddock, and David Currier. It's a dirty job, but somebody's got to do it! And finally, thanks to Wayne Erbsen for being a good humored and patient editor/publisher/husband.

Recipe Index

NATIVE GROUND MUSIC

BOOKS OF SONGS & LORE

Backpocket Bluegrass Songbook
Backpocket Old-Time Songbook
Cowboy Songs, Jokes, Lingo
   'n Lore
Crawdads, Doodlebugs &
   Creasy Greens
Front Porch Songs, Jokes & Stories
Log Cabin Pioneers
Old-Time Gospel Songbook
Railroad Fever
Rousing Songs of the Civil War
Rural Roots of Bluegrass

INSTRUCTION BOOKS

Bluegrass Banjo for the
   Complete Ignoramus!
Clawhammer Banjo for the
   Complete Ignoramus!
Painless Mandolin Melodies
Southern Mountain Banjo
Southern Mountain Dulcimer
Southern Mountain Fiddle
Southern Mountain Guitar
Southern Mountain Mandolin
Starting Bluegrass Banjo
   From Scratch

RECORDINGS

Authentic Outlaw Ballads
Ballads & Songs of the Civil War
Cold Frosty Morning
Cowboy Songs of the Wild Frontier
Front Porch Favorites
Log Cabin Songs
Old-Time Gospel Favorites
Pierre Cruzatte - Lewis & Clark
Raccoon and a Possum

Railroad Fever
Railroadin' Classics
Rural Roots of Bluegrass
Singing Rails
Songs of the Santa Fe Trail
Southern Mountain Classics
Southern Soldier Boy
The Home Front
Waterdance

Other great Native Ground cookbooks by Barbara Swell:

Children at the Hearth
Log Cabin Cooking
Mama's in the Kitchen
Old-Time Farmhouse Cooking
Take Two and Butter 'Em While They're Hot!
The Lost Art of Pie Making

Write or call for a FREE Catalog:

Native Ground Music
109 Bell Road
Asheville, NC 28805
(800) 752-2656

Email: **banjo@nativeground.com**
Web Site: **www.nativeground.com**